940.53
SITE

DATE DUE

8/97

LIBERATING THE GHOSTS

PHOTOGRAPHS AND TEXT FROM

THE MARCH OF THE LIVING

with Excerpts from the Writings of Participants

Raphael Shevelev

with

Karine Schomer

Foreword by
Michael Berenbaum
United States Holocaust Memorial Museum

LensWork Publishing
Portland, Oregon

FIRST EDITION

Softcover ISBN #1-888803-00-2
Hardcover ISBN #1-888803-01-0
Deluxe Limited Edition ISBN #1-888803-02-9
    includes original gelatin silver photograph printed by the author

Library of Congress Catalog Card Number: 96-75505

Published by LensWork Publishing, PO Box 22007, Portland, OR 97269
Printed in the United States of America

This volume is dedicated to the memory of
Moses Shevelev, a Jew,
from Libau, Latvia
and
Daniel Trocmé, a Huguenot,
from Le Chambon-sur-Lignon, France,
who together perished in Majdanek

FOREWORD

Pilgrimage is among the most ancient of religious acts. One journeys to, one journeys from. A part of all religions, it is essential to the story of the Jewish people.

"And the Lord said to Abraham, *Lech lecha*," meaning, in this context, "Go out of your land, the land of your birth, toward a place that I will show you." However, David Wolpe, following Hasidic commentary on the *Torah*, has suggested that *lech lecha* can have another, more radical meaning: *lech* means go; *lecha*, to yourself. We leave everything behind in search of the unknown, yet it is the great unknown, ourselves, that we take along.

Abraham went to Moriah with his beloved only son, Isaac. Ready to lose all, to abandon all, he gained all. Yet, we never again read of Abraham and Isaac together. One wonders how the narrative of pilgrimage would have read if seen through the eyes of the son.

Jacob concluded his life with a pilgrimage and a reunion with his favored son Joseph. His pilgrimage was fateful. His descendants were exiled and enslaved. Their eventual liberation was a pilgrimage, a journey into the unknown, to worship a God unknown. From slavery to redemption, from redemption to Sinai, from Sinai to the Promised Land. This was the pilgrimage of the people Israel, in ritual, in text, and in the lives of all their descendants.

In our generation, pilgrimage has returned as an essential religious act, along a new path. If an ancient generation went from Egypt to the Promised Land, we, their descendants, follow the tortured path of modern Jewish history from Auschwitz to Jerusalem.

For a long time no one dared. It was dangerous: the massacre of Jews in Kielce on July 4, 1946, the Polish anti-Semitic waves of

1957 and 1968, and the advent of communist rule, discouraged return. In the seventies, a few Jews went back, mostly to report that at Auschwitz there was no mention of Jews. The camp was portrayed as a place of Polish martyrdom. Such was my impression when I first went there in 1979 as a member of the delegation of the President's Commission on the Holocaust. Even the Jewish pavilion at Auschwitz, which was often closed, and unmentioned by local guides, was an inadequate representation of what had happened to the Jews. Alone among the barrack exhibitions, it seemed unrelated to its place in Auschwitz I. Only the magnificent monument of Treblinka, with its thousands of stone "sculptures," felt appropriate to the space, to the Event.

In the 1980s more people returned: survivors alone, children of survivors alone, children of survivors with their parents. With the ascent of Solidarity came an increased cultural tolerance and an awareness of the tourist value of these sites. More and more Jews came in search of a spark among the ashes. I returned time and time again, alone, with family, with colleagues, students, friends. What I found there — what we found there — helped shape the U.S. Holocaust Memorial Museum.

Israelis came to discover their own past. The generation of survivors returned for one more glimpse of their destroyed homes. Their grandchildren, touring the world after their service in the Israel Defense Force, came to find the unspoken secret of their existence. The extraordinary achievement of Israel, which had been a miracle to the grandparents, became an accepted fact for the children, and commonplace for the grandchildren. Only in Poland, amidst the rubble, could they really understand what Israel was: the miracle of rebirth.

The March of the Living unites Israeli and Diaspora youth to travel to Poland and encounter the evil, awful past. It is a march, a demonstration, an act of defiance. And though Polish authorities are cooperative, some anti-Semitic Poles occasionally harass these young Jews. Western Jews born in free and democratic countries, and Israeli Jews, who constitute a majority in their own country, come face-to-face with a venom they had not previously known, as they tour these places of death and destruction. They return strengthened in their resolve, more defiant, more confident, more determined.

Through these sensitive pictures, and the writings of the participants, you will share a glimpse of their experience, and have a sense of what awaits you on such a journey. Raphael Shevelev's stunning photographs, and the deeply expressive words of the youth, document a pilgrimage. They are an invitation to make a pilgrimage of your own. Raphael Shevelev and his wife Karine Schomer discovered themselves at Majdanek. *Lech lecha*, go — unto yourself.

My daughter Ilana went on a pilgrimage of her own, not as a student or a child, but as a teacher. She returned a different person, a deeper Jew. My son Lev went with me last year. Like the March of the Living, we went from Treblinka to the Western Wall. We stood among the dead in Treblinka, mourning, crying. We celebrated among the living in Jerusalem, praying, smiling. Such is the experience of the contemporary Jew. Such is the modern day pilgrimage.

The act of pilgrimage is also an act of hope. There is an ancient legend that the Messiah sits among the rubble of destruction. Perhaps! Perhaps!

Michael Berenbaum
Director, The Research Institute
U. S. Holocaust Memorial Museum
Washington, D.C.

ACKNOWLEDGMENTS

I knew from the beginning that a special pleasure awaited me: the joy of thanking the many people whose help and enthusiasm were indispensable to turning an idea into a reality. Seymour Fromer, Director of the Judah L. Magnes Museum, Berkeley, and curators Bill Chayes and Brad Berman were deeply involved in the evolution of the project. Gene Greenzweig, Executive Director of the Central Agency for Jewish Education, Miami, gave early encouragement and invaluable assistance all along the way. Mr. Greenzweig's colleague, Bobbi Kaufman, generously provided copies of the writings of American participants in the March. Yosef Kedem, Chairman of the Operations Committee of the March of the Living International (USA) traveled to California to discuss the project, arranged for our participation in the March, and provided continuous vital support; his assistant, Rhea Plottel, gracefully responded to our many requests for detailed information. Mickey Naggar-Bourne of the Bureau of Jewish Education, San Francisco and Zvi Weiss of the Bureau of Jewish Education, Los Angeles, gave us direct access to the California participants. For orienting us to Poland, we are indebted to Fred Rosenbaum, Director of Lehrhaus Judaica, Berkeley, and to Eva Golomb, who gave us an intimate picture of pre-war life in her native Cracow. Uri Zakai, General Director of the March of the Living International (Israel), who brilliantly coordinated the logistics of the March, made available necessary scheduling information and security clearance. Ralph Shedletsky of Willowdale, Ontario, who gave us seats on a Canadian delegation bus going to Treblinka, later arranged access to the writings of Canadian participants through Eli Rubenstein, National Director of the March of the Living (Canada). On our way to Poland, and on our return from Israel, we were grateful recipients of warm hospitality in the London home of Eddie and Pearl Bowman. As a photographer, I was blessed with advice from distinguished colleagues Morrie Camhi and Kim Komenich. Calmly ignoring my anxieties, Iris Davis of Davis Black & White meticulously processed my film. Brooks Jensen and Maureen Gallagher, the principals of LensWork Publishing, went far beyond their editorial roles, to become deeply engaged with the moral and artistic substance of this book.

The writings of the young participants in the March were often philosophically profound and poetically moving, and I am most grateful for permission to excerpt quotes from the several issues of the American *Reflections on the March of the Living* (Central Agency for Jewish Education, Miami) and of the Canadian *For You Who Died I Must Live On … Reflections on the March of the Living* (Mosaic Press, Oakville, Ontario).

This project was made possible by grants from the Dorot Foundation, the March of the Living Foundation, the Herman & Lee Vernekoff-Zuritsky Foundation, the Louis C. Stoumen Trust, a grant of materials from Ilford Ltd., and individual contributions from Dr. William and Lucie Alexander, Kenneth and Joyce Altshuler, Rev. Dr. Dale Bailey and Phyllis Bekemeyer, Dr. Edward and Dr. Pearl Bowman, Morrie and Lynn Camhi, John and Cecilia Chan, Dr. Nathan and Sylvia Cohen, Rev. Cynthia Crowner, Dr. Leo V. and Lucille Dos Remedios, Dr. Irene B. Fabrikant, Michael Freedland, Bud and Helen Gardner, Rev. Dr. James D. Glass, Prof. Michael and Nancy Gordon, Bert E. Green, Sharon Green, Dr. Robert and Kathleen Greene, Deborah Grossman and James Koenig, Prof. Austin and Patricia Hoggatt, Mark and Ginny Horlings, Dr. John Howarth and Dr. Faith Gabelnick, Norman and Valerie Johnson, Joell Jones, Sarah Kulberg, Richard and Catherine Larsen, Dennis and Pauline Lewak, Charles and Anne Mahnken, Jean-Paul and Joan Marx, Malcolm and Nora McGregor, Bernard and Harriet Miller, Dr. Sherwood Parker, Diana Richmond, Sir Gilbert and Lady Ines Roberts, Rev. Dr.

Andrew and Barbara Robinson, Richard and Barbara
Rosenberg, Rev. Dr. Howard and Elsie Schomer, David and
Jeanne Schwarz, Deborah Smaller, Rev. Dr. Archie and
Geraldine Smith, Dr. Michael Smith, Prof. Tatsuhiko and
Thuanna Tabara, George and Betty Thanos, Robbert van
Santen and Joanne Brem, Ambassador Tran Van-Thinh,
David and Denise Weinstein, Dr. Allen and Etta Winigrad.

I have kept for last the most special of all these acknowledg-
ments. My greatest debt and deepest gratitude go to my wife,
Karine Schomer, who was more than an equal partner in this
journey. This work could not have been accomplished
without her great intellect, her amazing logistical abilities, her
passion for the humanitarian significance of the project, and
her wholehearted contributions of expertise and loving
support, even at times when her own professional work was
severely demanding. She was there to hold me in Auschwitz.
She was there in every aspect of the labor, from conception to
completion. *Elle était toute entière.*

Raphael Shevelev
El Cerrito, California
December 10, 1995

Memorial candles on the dissection table, Majdanek

How many candles can we light to make their
    brief existence significant?
Is there any number enough, or just one
    emotion and a lifetime of dedication?
How can I perpetuate their six million dreams
    into my own?

Adina Frydman

Hope and
the March
Of The Living

Raphael Shevelev

I. At the end of 1945, as I was turning seven in that southern hemisphere summer, the first refugees from Europe began to arrive in Cape Town. On occasional Friday evenings, my father would bring back from his visit to the synagogue an individual or a couple newly arrived, in need of a meal or a bed until the community could find them home and work. I remember thinking that they all seemed anxious and excessively formal, and I was glad that I could understand and speak Yiddish. On a particularly hot night, just before Christmas, one such guest removed his jacket, then rolled up his sleeves, revealing a number on his arm. With a child's curiosity I walked around the table for a closer look, then asked him about his tattoo. I saw him look questioningly at my parents, and I saw my mother subtly shake her head. The question remained unanswered, as did my questions about relatives I had not known, but whose names I had heard spoken, and who had "disappeared." Later that evening, the same guest asked my father "When your son speaks English, can they hear that he is Jewish?" My father answered "No," and the man responded with a heartfelt "How fortunate!" that still pierces my soul. No more was said, and I soon forgot the incident. Five years later I became a member of the synagogue choir, and, again on a hot summer's night, the refugee Polish cantor, Jakob Lichterman, rolled up his shirtsleeves during rehearsal, and revealed a similar number on his forearm. This time there were no parents to shake their heads, and over the span of a few weeks, a powerful story emerged, and I learned that the cantor's life had been spared because of his beautiful lyric tenor voice: he was singing the *Sh'ma Yisrael*, "Hear, O Israel, the Lord our God, the Lord is One" on the way to the gas chamber when a Nazi officer "rescued" him to entertain German soldiers.

By the time I entered the University of Cape Town to read Politics, Philosophy and Economics, I had combed the libraries for literature on the Holocaust, and spent most of my freshman year getting more of an autodidactic education rather than the one my parents were paying for. It was a remarkable experience to study the depredations of racism while living in the South African social environment. Postgraduate study at the University of the Witwatersrand, Johannesburg, and at the Graduate School of International Studies, Denver, Colorado, eventually led me to the

University of California at Santa Barbara. There I introduced a course on race as a factor in international relations, an experience that deepened my perception of the links between racism and deliberate policymaking both within and among nations.

Much more recently, as a photographer and writer, I began to feel the need to produce a body of work as my own homage to the martyrs of the Holocaust, and the fiftieth anniversary of the liberation seemed a fitting time. I began to struggle with the shape and orientation of this work and nothing seemed quite appropriate. I didn't want to replicate the images of others: since the burial of the dead and the removal of the survivors from the concentration camps, there has been an enormous number of images made of the physical plant, the instruments of degradation and death. I had to draw something else from the abyss, and that something else found itself in the concept of hope. If, somehow, I could portray a seed of hope from the historical experience of catastrophe, then perhaps I could find my own peace in making some sense of the senseless, and thereby liberate my own ghosts.

I began to read again in earnest, Elie Wiesel, Viktor Frankl, Alan Bullock, Yehuda Bauer, Primo Levi, Raul Hilberg, Konnilyn Feig, Shlomo Breznitz, Michael Berenbaum, Rebecca Fromer…the list is as endless as it is distinguished. At last I came to a volume titled

Aspects of Hope, in which my own father-in-law, Dr. Howard Schomer, had been a contributor. It is one thing to write about hope, it is quite another to express it through photographs, and yet I knew conclusively that my work, if undertaken, would have to look to the future at least as much as to the past. There is a story by psychiatrist Viktor Frankl, himself a survivor, about the last moments of a young woman in his care, seeing in the window of her concentration camp hut a tree which "spoke" to her consolingly of eternal life. For a moment I had an inspiration: I would go to Auschwitz and photograph blossoming trees through the windows of the huts. However, many years ago I had been inoculated against *kitsch*, and that inspiration quickly joined many others in the special purgatory reserved for pathetic ideas and uninspired photography. After months of searching, I finally gave up, and in the relief of my own liberation, I indulged myself with a day-long stroll in the sun on my favorite Berkeley boulevard, Solano Avenue.

Coming out of Noah's Bagels, as I often do, I bought for the first time in a decade a copy of the *Jewish Bulletin of Northern California*, and sat on a bench to drink coffee and read. On the back page I found a large advertisement that read "On April Fourth 5,000 teenagers from 40 countries will meet in Poland for two weeks they will never forget: March of the Living." I rushed home, called the telephone number, and two days later the brochures appeared.

There was my project: to photograph the journey of young people, who are our hope and our future, as they face the evidence of the Holocaust. I would have the inestimable advantage of photographing reactions to the sites rather than only the sites themselves. For the next seventy-two hours, Karine and I went into seclusion and decided to document the pilgrimage, and I tried to compose myself sufficiently to propose an exhibition to Seymour Fromer, the founding Director of the Judah L. Magnes Museum in Berkeley. At the end of an hour of talking about the idea of the project to him and curator Bill Chayes, Seymour quietly said "Let's do it. We'll sponsor it and help raise the funds." Accustomed to waiting impatiently for curatorial committee decisions, I was shocked by his words. I asked him if he really meant it, and his response will continue to warm me for the rest of my life. He asked "If Beethoven came to ask you for help to raise the money for a new symphony, would you help him?" Speechless, I nodded yes, and he continued "Well, Mr. Beethoven, you're going to Poland!"

GHOSTS

"I remember, they once were here,"
    said the old man perched on an old red bench
    in front of the crumbling building.
"They ate different meat,
    and celebrated their holidays on different days.
They had a butcher and a baker down the street,
    but now their stores are all gone."
These people who used to live there,
    they are all gone, too.
"Big trucks came
    and took them all away.
They don't live here anymore."
Did he know that
    they don't live anywhere any more?

Launi Diamond

Grodzka Gate, Lublin, where street merchants
once filled the entrance to the Jewish town of Podzamce

As it began to rain, one of the students suggested they dance the *hora* ... the students linked hands and began circling in dance ... a dance of rebirth ... like the *menorahs* on the fence, the dancing in the square revived a lost culture.

Robin Shear

Szeroka Street, Cracow, once the central square of the Jewish town of Kazimierz.
Repeated pattern of the menorah forms the wrought iron fence, but the square is empty of any people.

We went to the Jewish cemetery, an entire culture gone, 250,000 gravestones, covered by weeds, leaves, forgotten. These people lived full lives, but the Holocaust stole their children. Now no one comes to clean their graves. I wish I could have done more, cleaned, washed, scrubbed.

Hilary Soule

Cmentarz Zydowski (Jewish Cemetery), Warsaw

When I visited the Jewish cemetery in Warsaw, I felt almost at peace. Here lay people who died because their lives were over, not because they were marched into the Tikocyn forest and murdered and not because they were deemed too weak to work.

Daniel Benel

Cmentarz Zydowski (Jewish Cemetery), Warsaw

A whisper of wings, a shadow of unsung songs. The roses that never bloomed, cures never found, lessons never taught.

Lauren Kerman

ścioro
iczą

t

ioro

em

Grandma Masha
had twenty

            grandchildren

Grandma Hana
had eleven

only I survived

 דים

isner   Jack Eisner   יזנר

*The Jewish Cemetery of Warsaw lies in a forest of tall, thin,
swaying, moaning trees, reflected in this plaque at the site of
the memorial to the one and a half million murdered children.*

"Those victims of man's hatred
    were children just like me
Those one and a half million innocent souls
    were children just like me
And you, who killed them
    you too were children just like me."

Jody Kasner

Children's Memorial, Jewish Cemetery, Warsaw

The square outside Cracow's synagogue is empty and the nearby graveyard is full. A synagogue that once swayed and sweated with prayer and song has become still with disuse, one of the "rare, preserved synagogues" spoken of in Polish tourist brochures. In other words, a relic.

Robin Shear

We walked through towns where Jewish communities once thrived, alive with synagogues and *yeshivas*. Now there are just shadows and whispers of what had once been.

Daryl Nierenberg

Cracow
Fifteenth century Old Synagogue, now a museum,
seen through the wrought-iron Star of David

Each night the Ariel Jewish Artistic Cafe in Cracow has a concert of Jewish and Russian music, and we returned that night to glory in the beauty of the Yiddish melodies from my youth — until I looked through the window at the dark, empty square, and realized that, save myself, there likely were no Jews either inside or outside the cafe. Fragments of the culture were being kept alive, but the people had disappeared. Are we more acceptable as nostalgia?

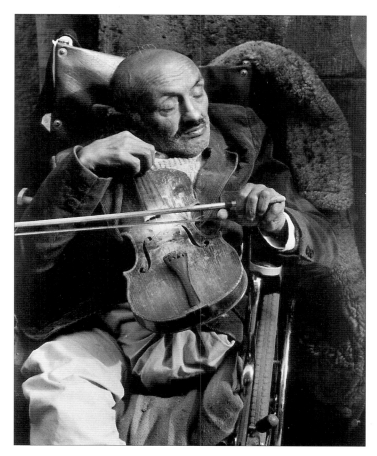

The streets of Cracow are also "home" to an impoverished old gypsy, a survivor, whose face glowed with the transformative power of the music from his battered fiddle.
I had seen that same expression on the face of Isaac Stern.

The synagogue was beautiful. The old *rebbe's* sermon was in Hebrew, but I felt I could understand; it was the universal language. All of us from our different backgrounds and countries could communicate. Had we not been there, there probably would not have been enough people to have a *minyan*.

Hilary Soule

Nozyk Synagogue, Warsaw: "Just a few old men," one of them said.

As I leaned forward to photograph this man in the Nozyk Synagogue, used as a stable by the Nazis, someone behind me said "*Er is nisht a Yid*" ("He is not a Jew"). "*Ober er hot a shaynem ponim,*" I responded ("But he has a beautiful face"). This Catholic friend had come to the synagogue on Passover to help complete the *minyan*, the quorum of ten men mandated by Jewish law for a worship service.

"The Tenth Man"

How can there not be concern about anti-Semitism? We were convinced that anti-Semitism perished here. Anti-Semitism did not perish. Its victims perished here.

Elie Wiesel

Prayer shawls, Nozyk Synagogue, Warsaw

II.   Poland came too soon. After so many years of hearing
       Polish Jewish folklore, after a lifetime of intermittent
       Holocaust study, after months of logistical preparation,
I so wanted the approach to be slow, a majestic unfolding of a past
blending into a present. Seemingly a moment after leaving a
pleasant stay in London, there was Warsaw under the port wing. I
had been warned about Polish antisemitism, and the historical
record suggests that it is not an empty warning, so I pinned the
silver March of the Living Star of David badge to my jacket lapel,
determined that I would not conceal, nor would I yield an inch.

Deliberately, Karine and I arrived in Poland a full week before the
participants in the March of the Living. I needed the time to
acclimatize and to look at the sites the young people would be
visiting. The planning and logistics had absorbed us so completely
in the few short months before the journey that I needed this time
also to think about the excellent counsel I had sought and had been
given by two friends who are also noted photographers: Morrie
Camhi, author of *The Prison Experience* and *Faces and Facets: The
Jews of Greece*, and Pulitzer Prizewinning photojournalist Kim
Komenich of the *San Francisco Examiner*. Both strengthened my
resolve to photograph from a particular point of view, rather than
to "cover" the event as a news photographer; to document, rather
than to react, and to do so by asking myself pertinent questions,

such as "Who are these young people and what do they intend to take home from the March of the Living? How can we help people understand the significance of the Holocaust for future generations?" Others cautioned me to "avoid the emotion and concentrate on the photography." I took that as an expression of affectionate concern, knowing it was advice I would not have the choice of taking, just as I knew that the nightmares would follow me home.

In 1939 there were 3.3 million Jews in Poland. Now there are about 25,000. They didn't emigrate. They were murdered, along with millions more who were sent from other parts of Europe to the Nazi death camps. My first task was to look at the remains of Jewish presence, and to me no image was of greater metaphorical impact than the photograph of a small park in the Jewish Quarter of Cracow. The iron fence is made in the repeated pattern of the *menorah*, the Jewish ritual candelabrum, but there is no human presence. Then the metaphor deepened. I found a vestige of life in that square by discovering the "Ariel Jewish Artistic Cafe," a warm haven from the cold outdoors, with tea and cake served by charming people. Each night the Ariel has a concert of Jewish and Russian music, and we returned that night to glory in the beauty of the Yiddish melodies from my youth — until I looked through the window at the dark, empty square, and realized that, save myself, there likely were no Jews either inside or outside the cafe. Fragments of the culture were being kept alive, but the people had disappeared. Are we more acceptable as nostalgia?

In Warsaw the disparity was even more painful. During Passover, which coincided with Holy Week, we visited the Nozyk Synagogue. The only one remaining in Warsaw, it had been used as a stable by the Germans, but is now restored to its original beauty. A few old men were conversing quietly after prayers, and as I bent to photograph one, a voice behind me said "*Er is nisht a Yid*" ("He isn't a Jew"). I responded "*Ober er hot a shaynem ponim*" ("But he has a beautiful face"). Then, on a hunch, I counted the worshipers. Together with the "beautiful face" there were just ten, a *minyan*, the quorum mandated by Hebrew law for a service. This Catholic friend had apparently come along to be the "tenth man," to make the service possible. We listened to their immensely tragic stories, and the great irony was that a South African-born American Jew, his American Protestant wife, and this deeply pathetic remnant of Polish Jewry had but one language in common: German, the language of the perpetrators.

That same night, along the elegant *Krakowskie Przedmiescie*, we followed a very large crowd into the music and light of the Holy Cross Church. There seemed to be a thousand worshipers, listening to the powerful, melodious voice of a priest standing near an urn containing the heart of Chopin. When I had been an infant, crowds of similar size would have packed the synagogues of Warsaw. Now, other than this one synagogue with its security door, there are only the tombstones among the moaning trees of the *Cmentarz Zydowski*, the Jewish cemetery on Okopowa Street, and the monuments. What had once been the ghetto has become a large, empty, grass-covered area surrounded by the brutalist architecture of Stalin-era apartment buildings, and presided over by a powerful, though equally brutalist, memorial. A few blocks away is the site of the *Umschlagplatz*, the place from which more than 300,000 Jews were shipped by train to the Nazi extermination camps.

It was time to take the train to Cracow. Cracow is a graceful and beautiful mediaeval city, known for its town square, Wawel Castle, the ancient Jagellonian University where Copernicus had been an undergraduate, and, in more recent history, for its proximity to Auschwitz and Plaszow, the concentration camp featured in *Schindler's List*. The streets of Cracow are also "home" to an impoverished, old gypsy, a survivor, whose face glowed with the transformative power of the music from his battered fiddle. I had seen that same expression on the face of Isaac Stern. On a beautiful, unseasonably warm day, when I could no longer tolerate my own apprehensive hesitancy, we walked down to the bus station and performed the most shockingly banal act of our lives: we bought bus tickets to Oswiecim (Auschwitz) as though we were buying tickets from Manhattan to Long Island. Ninety minutes later we were deposited on a pleasant avenue and the bus driver pointed vaguely to the right. With a sense of fearful anticipation, we entered hell-disguised-as-a-park, walking past the souvenir shop (we didn't investigate) and through the gate over which is preserved the iron, ultimately cynical sign *Arbeit Macht Frei* ("Work Liberates"). I now claim the distinction of being the only photographer in the world to have been at Auschwitz without photographing the entire sign. But I did use the reversed word *Frei* ("Free") to indicate the status of a young woman entering the camp. Another sign, supremely ironic, caught my attention. It was on the outside of the once electrified barbed wire, and meant to warn German personnel: *Vorsicht … Lebensgefahr* ("Caution … Mortal Danger").

On the flight from Heathrow to Warsaw a very intoxicated young English businessman, in a moment of lucidity, had warned us about Auschwitz, saying "It's always cold." In the brilliant sunshine of that day we were relieved to see him wrong, until we walked into Block 5, and felt that we had entered a refrigerator, one that contains mounds of hair, spectacles, shoes, brushes and other personal effects stolen from the doomed. "The most common objects/ of our everyday/ become a desecration," wrote poet Daniel

Siegal. For many of the march participants, the mounds of shoes took on a special significance, perhaps because they are artifacts both so personal and yet so universal. Chava Shimon was later to write "Which shoes liked to walk? Which shoes liked to dance? Each pair travelled a different path, but they all ended in the same horrific destination." In a moment of touchingly personalized insight, she added "Each lock of hair had a head, and each head had a mind. Each mind had dreams, hopes and beliefs …"

To restore my own sanity I walked to the end of a corridor and forced open a rusty window to sun-warmed air. Beneath me, at ground level, was a most incongruous sight, a wooden bench not unlike those I'd seen in California parks. Rebecca Fromer later reminded me of an incident described in her book, *The Holocaust Odyssey of Daniel Bennahmias, Sonderkommando*. A German officer recognized a prisoner sent for execution as being a singer whose voice had given him much pleasure in concerts before the war. He guided her to a bench, they talked about music, he gave her a cigarette, and then he shot her.

Along this path of suffering and death over 300,000 Jews were driven in 1942-1943 from the Warsaw Ghetto to the gas chambers of the Nazi extermination camps.

Inscription at the Umschlagplatz

Umschlagplatz: the embarkation point from the Warsaw Ghetto
to the death camps

"What was their crime?" I asked a friend.

"Their only crime was being Jewish," she replied.

Hayley Becker

And to each of them I will give a name and a monument
To every man, to every woman, to every child
And to each of them I will give a name and a monument
To those who fought and to those who had no way to fight
To those who sang on the way to their deaths
And to those who were silent.

Aviva Goldberg

Umschlagplatz: the names

We pay tribute to their lives,
not only to their deaths.

Noam Samson

Warsaw Ghetto Uprising Monument,
Warsaw

(detail)

On a beautiful, unseasonably warm day, when I could no longer tolerate my own apprehensive hesitancy, we walked down to the bus station and performed the most shockingly banal act of our lives: we bought bus tickets to Oswiecim (Auschwitz) as though we were buying tickets from Manhattan to Long Island.

Bus ticket to Auschwitz, Holocaust Memorial Day

Beneath me, at ground level, was a most incongruous sight, a wooden bench not unlike those I'd seen in California parks. Rebecca Fromer later reminded me of an incident described in her book, *The Holocaust Odyssey of Daniel Bennahmias, Sonderkommando*. A German officer recognized a prisoner sent for execution as being a singer whose voice had given him much pleasure in concerts before the war. He guided her to a bench, they talked about music, he gave her a cigarette, and then he shot her.

Birkenau was huge. I marched through the front gate only to find that it was another mile to the other end of the camp and it was twice as wide as that. There seemed to be no end to it. I began to wonder. The Nazis had dozens of these camps. With the space, time, energy and resources they had, how could they have failed at their task of destroying the Jews?

Benjamin Andron

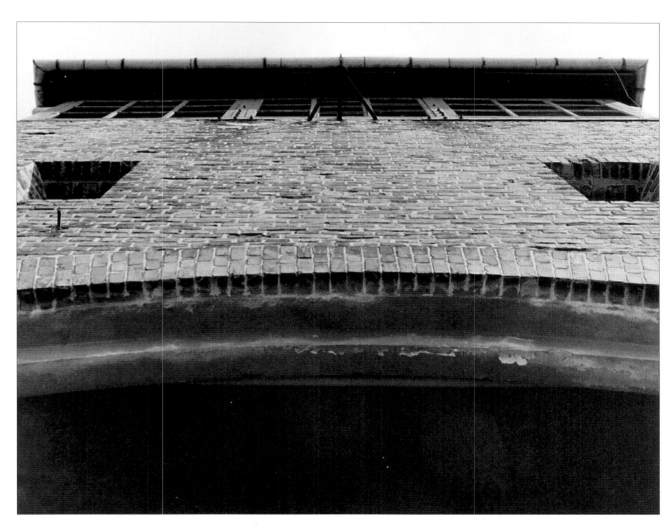

The mouth of Birkenau

Sometimes when I hear a train pass by
I am there
Returned to the tracks that chilled my soul.
Is that the whistle of the train or the screams of
the helpless?
Sometimes I pray
For silence.

Elyse Korman

Trains, trains, more trains!
Chugging hastily across Europe.
Listen.
Here they come.

Michael Passon Marcus

End of the line, Birkenau

A number.
J3602A4.
That's all she was.
Penned up within
The barbed wire.
I saw her
When I journeyed there
To Auschwitz.
She tried to tell me,
Yet I wouldn't hear.
A number, she explained,
Takes everything away.
Beginning with your name.
A number …
J3602A4 has whispered her story
To me
Day by day, hour by hour,
Since I abandoned her grave.
The agony, the dehumanization,
The loss of dignity,
The loss of identity.
To be a number

Is the beginning
Of hell.
She whispers, from across
The barbed wire,
Eyes darting from side to side.
Terrified still.
A number is the way
Jailers begin the
Torture.
J3602A4 no longer has a
Name.
Yet I have named her.
Chaya Shulamit.
I see her reflection every time
I look in
The mirror.
She is I
I live for both of us.

Carrie Bacher

Lamps of darkness

As I enter the barracks, a wind slams the door behind me, and my memorial candle goes out. I walk past row after row of wooden bunks, now decaying and falling apart. I stop in the light of a window to take a picture. But a voice behind me makes me turn around.

Hello.

I'm sorry. Are you speaking to me?

Yes.

Forgive me. Do I know you?

Yes.

How?

You remember me.

From when?

A long time ago, yet not so long ago.

May I ask your name?

Names are irrelevant in this place. But you may ask my number.

What shall I call you if I don't know your name?

You needn't call me anything. I'll always be with you.

Are you alive?

In you I am alive.

I don't understand. What do you mean?

Mean? I mean sadness, desperateness, cruelty, craziness! But because of you I also mean hope.

What do you hope for?

To be remembered. That's all I ever hope for. If you remember me and yourself, it can't happen again.

What happened to you?

I died, in a gas chamber. My little sister still holding my hand.

I have a little sister.

I know.

From where do you get your hope?

From the warmth I can still feel from her hand. From a kind word received from a non-Jew, a supportive hug from a friend.

Not from God?

What God?

The God of your people. Our people. The God our ancestors believed in for thousands of years.

Give me a reason why I should believe in Him.

Because some survived.

I didn't.

But some did.

You have much to learn, my little friend.

About what?

About life. And death. I have trouble justifying the death of six million by the saviour of a few. Yes, it is true. Judaism still carries on. As it always has. As it always will. But why? To what God do they pray?

You are bitter.

Tell me I do not have the right to be bitter.

I cannot. But I have a question.

I have many questions.

How do you explain survivors if you do not believe in God?

People.

Pardon?

The goodness of a few people saved others. Not God. Why would God save us? He had nothing to lose. No friends, no family, no neighbours or co-workers.

He lost his worshipers.

Not all of them. There are many who still believe.

But by not believing, you let them win!

Who?

The Nazis. They wanted to destroy your faith, and they have.

No. They destroyed me. God destroyed my faith.

Suddenly the image flickered as wind blew through an open window.

Wait! I have so much more to ask you!

I have but one answer for you. Listen to the wind that scatters the ashes and at the same time, warms the spirit. Remember me. Remember us. Live the life we never had a chance to. Remember, remember, remember.

It echoes in the air as I turn and leave the barracks. But I do not shut the door behind me. And the wind is at my back.

Jennifer Trehearne

Prisoner barrack at Birkenau

There was nothing left to see there but rows of empty, echoing barracks, and the only odour was the clinging smell of fear.

Lori Sugarman

Majdanek is a place of the most utter desolation, devoid of the vivification of trees or topographical grace. It is well preserved, largely in the condition in which the Germans left it before fleeing from the Soviet Army. Grass now covers the ground among the huts, but it didn't then: the prisoners had eaten it all.

Why was Majdanek the most haunting of all the camps we visited? Perhaps because it was so well preserved it could be operational given sixteen hours notice, or maybe it was the row of apartment houses just across the road from the gas chamber.

Noah Oppenheim

Majdanek — a mammoth urn with a raised roof …

Majdanek was an extermination camp located right inside the city of Lublin. A crematorium and an apartment house can be photographed in the same picture.

Hilary Soule

There was a mountain of ashes taken from the crematoria. Perhaps one of my relatives is among those ashes.

Keren Lazarow

... containing a huge mound of human ash

A mother holding her child … she stands between barracks in a concentration camp, holding her baby as high as she can in a futile attempt to save her child.

Anabela Moskovitz

The grass will talk.
The barracks will tell us.
The dust will whisper its story.

We will see.
Then we will talk.
And we will March on.
We shall live on.

Marni Beth Birnbaum

To prepare for the entry into Auschwitz,
a young man clothes himself in the flag of a democracy.

The Nazis aim, shoot, the man dies. He fervently wishes there was an intervening force to save him — or maybe he just wants the despair to be over. Now maybe thirty of us marchers stand here and I want to shout to his spirit "I am here! I am standing in the way of the gunmen. I am intervening!" But I am fifty years too late and what can I do for your life? I know I can teach your legacy, your story.

Penina Rantz

Facing the execution wall, Auschwitz

They lined us up for the march by countries. Once we got to our station, I looked up and saw the barrack's number: Block 10, the barrack in which they did medical experiments on women. Words can't express the emotions I felt at that moment.

Sherry Sherman

*A group of American women stand before Block 10,
Auschwitz, where Luftwaffe physician Horst Schumann
performed surgical "experiments" on Jewish women.*

We have lit
an everlasting candle
with each tear we've cried.

Shayna Levine

At Block 10, Auschwitz

There is a sea of stones here
Placed over shattered dead earth
Rough-edged and ripped from their places
Each one a symbol of a town, a city
And those who were stolen from it.

More died here each day than there are people I know
More died here finally than there are people I will ever know
What did this help?
How could this massacre of the innocent
Have done anyone any good?

As my body wanders through the maze
The very stones cause me to stumble
Like desperate, withered hands
Clawing at me
Dragging me down
Not out of malice
But because they are so cold
So lonely
So empty.

Josh Culbertson

Remembrance among the 17,000 stones commemorating lost communities, Treblinka

Then I saw a bird. I remembered the poem *The Birds Don't Sing in Treblinka*. Not knowing why, my feet followed this bird as it took flight. Suddenly, the bird disappeared. Awakened to my surroundings, I gasped: the stone in front of me was quite large, and it read "Opoczon." This is it, this was my grandparents' home town. For the first time in my life, I felt connected. I came from somewhere. I belong. I am alive. And though the birds don't sing, and the stones stand silently for the world to see, I remember, and so should we all.

Anabela Moskovitz

Ashen limbs green
Among greening pine trunks
Seething with brown sap
Yearning to be the richest amber,
In whose reflection lies
The strawberry field,
Beside the ashfields,
of Treblinka.

Val Vinokurov

Mother and son at Treblinka

How is it that only fifty years have passed
and I can sit in Springtime
staring at a pit once full of bodies,
but now full with charred rocks, flowers and candles?

Caroline Libman

I'm lucky my grandparents left Poland
and went to the United States.

Steven Helft

The ovens in Majdanek still have ashes in them. I waited until everyone had left the room, then I put my hand in the ashes. It was something I knew I needed to do ... I wondered if it was disrespectful; I wondered if I was disturbing those souls. But how could it be disrespectful? I felt I was caressing them, letting them know someone was here.

Sherry Sherman

Coming out of the crematorium, Majdanek

There will be better days
Live them for me.
This is my message to you,
I died, but I never gave up hope.
Hope, hope …
Life, life …
I am alive in you,
And you will smile for another day.

Jennifer Trehearne

Crematorium, Majdanek
Photograph of the Shevelev family, circa 1920.
Moses, second from right, later a student at the Sorbonne,
was deported to Majdanek and murdered in 1944.

How can we take in what
is unfathomable? It is like
trying to swallow glass, or
breathe without air.

Robin Shear

"Magnified and Sanctified be His Great Name … "
The words of the Mourners' Kaddish recited in Majdanek.
The Polish inscription reads "Let Our Fate Be A Warning For You."

I prayed that day as I've never prayed before. We sang *Hatikvah* and I could have sworn I heard voices coming out of the chimney of the crematorium.

Merissa Schuk

A prayer for life, a prayer for death ... a prayer
to remember those who have died ... a prayer
to assuage mourners ... a prayer for those parents whose children died before they could
mourn their mothers and fathers ... a prayer
to mourn for those children whose parents
died before they could mourn the loss of in-
nocence ... a prayer to remember the candles
that were extinguished before they burnt out
... a prayer to remember our candles ... a
prayer to remember violence ... a prayer to
rekindle the flame ...

Becky Levin

III. A week later, on *Yom Hashoah*, Holocaust Memorial Day, almost seven thousand people met at Auschwitz for the event that gives the March of the Living its name: a march in silence for the three kilometers from Auschwitz to the gas chambers of Birkenau, a symbolic evocation of what had once been the marches of death. The march was led by two hundred survivors, though, as Miriam Naylor, a young participant, later wrote: "Survivors of Death, maybe, but the Holocaust? No, no one survived the Holocaust." During the previous night the rain had turned to snow, giving the statues of Cracow white perukes and epaulettes. It now added an appropriately frigid atmospheric appearance to the barracks of Auschwitz.

As the march began to form, the most astounding and unforgettable sight was the mass of flags bearing the Star of David within the perimeter of Auschwitz, and the most unforgettable sounds were those of the *shofar*, the ram's horn, and the Hebrew lament, *Kol Nidrei*, customarily sung three times on the eve of *Yom Kippur*, the Day of Atonement. Now it was being played on a single unaccompanied violin, every note clearly articulated in the cold stillness, by Jacques Stromza, a survivor who had been forced to play in the camp orchestra fifty years earlier. For Launi Diamond, the music "wasn't a tune," but rather a violin's cry that "told us to tell its story to the world." At the last moment, the final group to join the march entered the camp: the Polish Friends of Israel, a group of Gentiles the oldest among whom had been rescuers of Jewish lives. One of their continuing, dedicated tasks has been to find the "hidden children," those lodged with, and saved by, Polish Gentiles, and to offer them the opportunity of reconnecting to Judaism. Among these marchers, an elderly woman, Halina Ostik, was pointed out to me as their founder. When I asked her "Are you the founder?" she smiled and shook her head gently. "No, God is the Founder." It took a while before I could see clearly through the viewfinder again.

In complete silence, the thousands of the March of the Living covered the three kilometers to the notorious architecture of the entrance to Birkenau, the largest of the death camps. As they approached the gate, many broke from the line of the march to light memorial candles on the railway lines, so that the last fifty yards of steel seemed to glitter under grey skies. A number of the marchers brought wooden plaques, perhaps a foot long, on which names of lost loved ones had been inscribed, and they were planted in a field within Birkenau, as a "cemetery," close to the end of the railway line. For all whose names were inscribed, and for so many others, it had been literally the end of the line.

The close contact with the young people, as well as with groups of adults from all over the world, gave us a window into the range of their intellectual and emotional reactions. Some remained grimly silent, some seemed nonchalant, but the vast majority of every age allowed their raw emotions and their ideas to flow freely and to draw strength from them and each other. Judging from the writings of previous participants in the March of the Living — this was the fourth biennial event — most of them regard their experiences as life-altering. Among the survivors there were those for whom this journey brought a measure of needed closure, and a few for whom it again opened old and terrifying wounds.

There are two sites which could now not possibly be more different from each other, despite the grim commonality of their purpose: Treblinka and Majdanek. The lyrical-sounding Treblinka is situated a little more than an hour's drive northeast of Warsaw, and, as it is difficult to reach with public transportation, we were given a ride in one of the buses of the Canadian delegation. Hidden behind a knoll among rural woods, well shielded from prying eyes, the camp became one of the Nazis' most efficient killing fields, brought to an end by a desperate prisoner revolt, but not before 800,000 had been murdered there. Nothing of the camp itself remains, but in a large clearing, the Polish government has erected a monument of immense power, more than 17,000 uncut stones of various sizes, each representing the loss of an entire community. We watched the young people walk silently among the stones, and every once in a while a cry indicated that someone had found the stone commemorating a lost community from which their family had been deported. As I knelt to photograph behind a stone large enough to conceal me, I heard, coming from the other side, the voice of a survivor, speaking in Polish-accented Yiddish, telling his murdered mother about her wonderful grandchildren. I remained kneeling for a long time, unwilling to disturb his privacy and needing the time to compose myself.

Majdanek is located in eastern Poland, in the city of Lublin, which was for centuries a spiritual center for Jews. The *Yeshiva*, the rabbinical college, once a great place of learning, is now a disastrously dilapidated and primitive Polish medical school. Here in Lublin the Nazis made no attempt to hide their "work." Majdanek is on an urban bus line, less than five kilometers from the center of town. It was "the only large Nazi camp constructed in the midst of things, without secrecy or subterfuge" wrote Konnilyn Feig. It is a place of the most utter desolation, devoid of the vivification of trees or topographical grace. It is well preserved, largely in the condition in which the Germans left it before fleeing from the Soviet Army. Grass now covers the ground among the huts, but it didn't then: the prisoners had eaten it all.

Commanding a view of the camp are two major structures: the crematorium with its intact ovens and dissection table, on which March of the Living participants placed hundreds of memorial candles; and a monument designed by sculptor Wiktor Tolkin as a mammoth urn with a raised roof, containing a huge mound of human ash. Karine and I had come to Majdanek not only because it was on the itinerary of the March of the Living. For us it was a very personal pilgrimage. Karine grew up in the French resistance village of Le Chambon-sur-Lignon, where the Huguenot villagers, under the leadership of Pastor André Trocmé, had committed a "conspiracy of goodness," saving the lives of thousands of Jews under the noses of the SS. The pastor's second cousin, Daniel Trocmé, had been the supervisor of a children's home when the Nazis found Jewish children concealed by him among the others. Daniel refused to be parted from "his" children, and was deported to Majdanek, where he was murdered. When the Nazis entered Paris my uncle Moses Shevelev was a student at the Sorbonne. He was also deported to Majdanek, where he too was murdered. Our first visit to Majdanek, prior to the arrival of the March, occurred on Easter Monday, April 4th, 1994. On this holiday in a devoutly Catholic country, the camp was deserted, and we found ourselves the only visitors there. In a private ceremony, we lit candles. Months after this event, while searching through documentation,

I discovered that we had been there on an anniversary: Daniel Trocmé had been murdered exactly fifty years earlier, on April 4th, 1944.

Balancing my memory of Majdanek's cold, overwhelming desolation are the mental and photographic images of the responses of the March of the Living participants: exploring the camp with a mixture of strength and sadness, with questions and with determination, reciting in harmony the mourners' *Kaddish*, repeating, even in that place, the words of faith, "Magnified and Sanctified be His great Name …" I am also reminded of the survivor who told me that he may yet learn to forgive the Germans, but wondered if he could ever forgive God. Elie Wiesel recounts that on April 11, 1945, the *Kaddish* recited upon the liberation of Buchenwald was a thanksgiving, but also an outcry: "Why did You not spare so many others?" That same private, agonizing conflict between faith and angry despair erupted in Jennifer Trehearne's questions: "Then where was He? His people, His creations, were suffering as no one deserves to suffer … And God watched silently. People cried. And God listened. But did He hear?…Where was God? I have to question."

HOPE

I walked under the sign at the entrance to Auschwitz that says *"Arbeit Macht Frei."* But I saw the sign twice, once when I entered and once when I exited. People who were sent to Auschwitz fifty years ago saw the sign only once.

Meredith Grossman

Perhaps I am the only photographer in the world to have visited Auschwitz and not to have photographed the entire sign *"Arbeit Macht Frei"* ("Work liberates"). But I did want to use the word *"Frei"* ("Free") to describe the status of the young woman entering the camp.

We took our places among the 7,000 marchers for the silent trek from Auschwitz to Birkenau. Marching in front of me was a group of survivors. As I watched them I tried to imagine the courage that it must take to return to a place where they had been through hell on earth.

Jon Kaufthal

I am here for them
To show them what we are now.

Debra Weintraub

Auschwitz, Poland, 1943: A young Jewish woman named Sophia, in her twenties, trudged down a dirt road. A wife and mother, she had no idea where her husband and child were. She never found out, because she never left Auschwitz.

Auschwitz, Poland, 1990: A young Jewish woman named Sophia, in her twenties, trudged down a dirt road. A wife and mother, she knew her husband and child were safe and that she would walk out of Auschwitz to freedom and security.

Walking into Auschwitz on the March of the Living, I made a vow to my grandmother and to myself that I would somehow make up for what was stolen from all of us.

Sophia Fischer

The Torah in Birkenau

"You see? I always have a smile on my face. There may be tears in my eyes, but I will always smile."

Irving (Yitzchak) Eisner

As we were leaving Auschwitz, a small group of Polish people stood cheering us on. They carried a banner reading "Polish Friends of Israel." I began to have faith in all people. Someday the world will come to see the stupidity of hate.

Chantal Abitbol

I walked up to Halina Ostik.
"Are you the founder of the Polish Friends of Israel?" I asked.
She smiled and shook her head gently, "No, God is the Founder."

Survivor, Irving (Yitzchak) Eisner

Rescuer, Halina Ostik

In our blue jackets we marched as one, marched against dehumanization, marched against the past, marched toward the future.

Debbie Roth

To put numbers in perspective, it is notable that the 7,000 people who marched from Auschwitz to Birkenau seemed like such a large number, but in fact it represented not much more than one-fourth of one day's arrivals in Treblinka, all of whom would be killed on the very day that they arrived.

Leo Schwartzberg

We marched, six thousand of us, in those identical blue jackets, arms linked in lines of six, marched silently, united, across dirty snow, from the barracks of Auschwitz to the gas chambers of Birkenau. Two and a half miles that our grandparents and relatives were once commanded to walk in icy cold without the warm coats and sturdy shoes we were wearing. We walked for them, the six million who were massacred simply for being Jewish.

Daryl Nierenberg

Reflecting the ghosts

In complete silence, the thousands of the March of the Living covered the three kilometers to the notorious architecture of the entrance to Birkenau, the largest of the death camps. As they approached the gate, many broke from the line of the march to light memorial candles on the railway lines, so that the last fifty yards of steel seemed to glitter under grey skies.

Approaching Birkenau

When Irene returned to windswept Auschwitz, fifty years later as a participant in the March of the Living, I was there to witness one of her miracles. She was determined to locate the exact spot where she last saw her family and there light her candle. When she thought she had found it, where the train tracks ended, she struck her match, but the trashing wind blew out the flame. Saddened by her failure to complete her mission, she began to cry. Then, as a last attempt, thinking maybe that was not the right place, she moved over one foot and lit her candle. The flame caught, fought the wind, and proceeded to glow all day.

Dori Kaplan

Since the victims did not have their own individual graves and gravestones, in a field we each placed a small wooden plaque with the names of people who died there. I wrote the names of Lilly and Julian Strauss, my great-grandparents. I wondered, who gave Hitler the right to take away my father's grandparents?

Eric Lamm

Saba, I erected a gravestone for you in Birkenau.

Noam Samson

The March ended deep inside Birkenau. Atop the rubble of destroyed crematoria, where Jews once died, Jews now prayed. We sang and we chanted and recited the prayers that were once spoken by those who perished. We let our spirits climb and our hopes soar as we prayed together.

Daryl Nierenberg

Memorial ceremony, Birkenau

I hold the hand of a friend tightly, biting my lip and trying to take in all that I see. Several yards away I can see a caved-in brick construction: a crematorium. Atop this building stands a group of people, all wearing blue jackets and waving Israeli flags.

Sharit Ingber

As a survivor of one of the deadliest camps, I revisited my dreadful childhood, as well as the gas chamber where I lost everyone in my family and almost became ashes myself. I went down under the rubble where the crematorium was in Birkenau and scraped up the ashes that are still there from the Holocaust. I took the ashes with me to Israel and buried them in *Yad Vashem*. I do not hate today because of what happened to me. I am just very sad that there is still so much hate in the world in spite of what the world saw.

Irene Zisblatt

Above the cremetorium ruins, Birkenau

IV. The resurgence of faith and the renascence of hope came with the transformative flight from glacial Poland to the luminous warmth of Israel. No country is responsible for its weather, and it is well to remember that Poland suffered deeply from the Nazi aggression that also crafted it into the graveyard of European Jewry. The climatic shift is nevertheless a metaphor that exceeds the meteorological. It is emblematic of the contrast between the snowy march to the spiritual emptiness of Birkenau, and the spiritual regenesis of the pilgrimage to the Western Wall. It is in the distinction between *Yom Hashoah* and *Yom Ha'Atzmaut* — Holocaust Memorial Day and Israel Independence Day. Dara Horn chose trees to symbolize the transition, from those in the village of Tikocyn, where all the Jews were murdered in the forest,

> The trees that towered above
> like aloof distracted sentries,
> their branches turned away from you

to the tree she planted in Jerusalem:

> I would like to promise everyone that this tree
> will live as long as a tree ever can,
> even when there is no longer such a thing
> as a tree or a person who looks away
> when someone cries for help.
> This tree will never turn away.

Finally, it was Hilary Soule who so exuberantly expressed the sense of hope and renewal:

> On *Yom Ha'Atzmaut* I danced in the street, did the *hora* in the streets of Jerusalem. It filled me with such joy. I ran with the children, bopped people's heads with funny plastic hammers, threw confetti, danced with people from around the world. Danced with an Israeli soldier. Met people from London. Sang in the street. Saw the most Jews I have ever seen. Ate *felafel*, danced and celebrated. The people of Israel live!

After the publication of his sensitive book *In The Camps*, which he authored as a *Liebesdienst*, a service of love, Erich Hartmann wrote to me:

> The central and greatest difficulty of remembering, not only with this particular fiftieth anniversary but with life experiences generally, is to transmit events that are perforce intensely personal, to others who cannot have anything but *knowledge*, without the flavor, without the fear or joy of what was then an intense present and is now the inevitably fading past.

Hartmann is right of course: generations born after unique and cataclysmic events cannot have the *primary* experience of those events. And yet, as I observed the faces and the reactions of the Marchers, my impressions were of young people attempting to acquire something deeper and more profound than intellectual insight, using their minds, yes, but also uniting their emotional receptivity with their ability to identify, and thus trying to reach beyond knowledge, to *understanding*. Their experience was not primary, but it was a deep and certainly life-altering one that stands on an elevated bridge between knowledge and being, and brings the two closer together. This is the particular genius and the gift of the March of the Living. One doesn't fully learn history, about history, or from history, until it touches the soul.

The March of the Living initially evolved from ideas about promoting Holocaust education among the young by the Hon. Avrom Hirschson, a member of the *Knesset*, Israel's unicameral parliament. The services of Dr. Shmuel Rosenman, Head of Secondary Education for the municipality of Tel Aviv, were secured, and in 1987 Dr. Rosenman came to the United States to seek the cooperation of American Jewish educators, including Dr. Alvin Schiff, then Executive Vice President of the Board of Jewish Education of New York, and Gene Greenzweig, Executive Director of the Central Agency for Jewish Education in Miami. The late Walter Hess, former Executive Vice President of the United Israel Appeal of Canada and Shlomo Shimon, Executive Director of Montreal's Jewish Education Council, were instrumental in gaining acceptance for the March of the Living in Canada. The first March of the Living took place in 1988 — the forty-fifth anniversary year of the Warsaw Ghetto Uprising — with fifteen hundred participants from fifteen countries. It was followed biennially by Marches in 1990, 1992, and 1994, and has since become an annual event of over five thousand participants from more than forty countries. The intense preparatory educational and administrative work, and the immensely complex logistics, are the responsibilities of a deeply dedicated corps of international volunteers. First conceived as a message to Jewish youth worldwide, the March of the Living, through its growing numbers of participants, including those who are not Jewish, conveys a powerfully humanistic message to the world. It is a *Hoffnungsdienst*, a service of hope.

The March of the Living makes a singular contribution to the universal idea that the ghosts of the martyrs remain imprisoned by the continuing wars and genocides of our century, and that it is the responsibility of ensuing generations to liberate the ghosts by putting an end to the terror, the intolerance, and the suffering. The generation of the March of the Living is the last generation to have direct contact with the survivors of the Holocaust. It is their task to take the living story into future history. There is both a story and a message. The story is the province of historiography, but it is in the *message* that we find the seeds of hope. Nowhere is this better expressed than in the inscription on the monument at Majdanek: "Let Our Fate Be A Warning For You." In the acceptance of that injunction lies profound hope, and the liberation of the ghosts.

You are our link with the past
We are your hope for the future.
We borrowed strength from you
You put your faith in us.
You showed us it is possible to love,
In spite of all the hate you have seen.
You showed us strength and courage
We thought not possible.

Michael Leeman

At Yad Vashem, *in Jerusalem, the sandstone has been
excavated to become a canyon in the form of the map of
Europe. It is known as the Valley of the Lost Communities.*

As I stood next to the *Kotel* with my hands upon its wall, I listened, absorbed, imagined, remembered, and prayed. Standing there, a flood of warmth and comfort filled my body. I was in Israel. I was safe.

Sarah Marlin

The first time I went to the Western Wall I was told by one of the rabbis that you get from the Wall what you bring to it. I was bringing a loss of faith in humanity, anger, confusion, and sadness. As I walked up to the Wall, I looked with amazement at the holiest place in the world for the Jews. At that moment all my anger, confusion and depression left me. As I looked around at all the people praying I began to have faith in humanity again.

Sara Marks

Praying at the Western Wall, Jerusalem

To remember the past
To live in the present
To trust in the future

Abba Kovner

Inscription in the entrance to the
Diaspora Museum, Tel Aviv

To you who tell me that it is over,
 that I have left the pain of Poland,
 to you who tell me to "get over it" and "move on"
 because I am home now,
 I have something to tell you.
Just because I stand in front of you,
 because you can see me,
 because you can reach out
 and touch me because I am home,
 does not mean that I am so far from that piercing pain.
You may think that the pain of Poland
 is halfway across the world,
 that it is still in the death camps,
 contained within the barbed wire.
Well, I have news for you.
That pain has travelled with me from Poland to Israel
 and now it has come home with me.
So don't tell me that because I am home
 I can no longer feel the pain.
To forget their pain is to inflict it once more.
So please, now that I am home, understand that once in a
 while I will still feel
 the tears, the trembling, the pain and the arms
 that rushed to embrace me.
Thank God for those arms,
 for without them the pain
 would have swallowed me whole.
I will never forget any of this, and please, don't ask me to,
 because for me the March of the Living will never be over.

Yona Shem Tov

Further information on the March of the Living may be obtained at the following addresses:

Dr. Shmuel Rosenman, Chairman
Avi Dickstein, Liaison with the United States
March of the Living (International)
6 Laskov Street
Tel Aviv
Israel 64736
Tel: 03-696-6161
Fax: 03-691-8962

Yosef Kedem, Executive Vice-Chairman
March of the Living (USA)
136 East 39th Street
New York, NY 10016
U. S. A.
Tel: 212-252-0900
Fax: 212-252-0474

Eli Rubenstein, National Chairman
March of the Living (Canada)
4600 Bathurst Street
Suite 315
Willowdale, ONT M2R 3V3
Canada
Tel: 416-636-7655
Fax: 416-636-9897

RAPHAEL SHEVELEV was born in South Africa and came to the United States in 1964 as a Fulbright-Hayes grantee. After studies at the Graduate School of International Studies in Denver, he taught political science and international relations at the University of California's Santa Barbara and Davis campuses. In 1989, following a lifelong dream, he made a career change to become an arts professional in photography. He has taught at the Ansel Adams Center, the Richmond Art Center, The Center for Photographic Art, Carmel, and the San Francisco Art Institute, and he is currently adjunct professor in the Department of Humanities and Creative Arts at Golden Gate University, San Francisco. His photographs and/or writings on photography have been published in *Image Magazine, Art of California, Photo Metro, SouthWestArt, The Photographic Journal, Contemporary Photography, Artweek, The Monthly, Connections, LensWork Quarterly,* and elsewhere. He is the author of the text in *Wynn Bullock: The Enchanted Landscape, Photographs 1940-1975* (New York: Aperture, 1993). In his photodocumentary work, Mr. Shevelev brings the influences of his social science background to his sensibilities as an artist.

KARINE SCHOMER, born in Philadelphia, Pennsylvania in 1944, grew up in the resistance village of Le Chambon-sur-Lignon, France and French-speaking Switzerland. She was schooled at the Collège Cévenol in Le Chambon and at the Collège de Nyon in Switzerland before returning to the United States. She is a graduate of Oberlin College in European History and French literature, and later received her MA in history and PhD in South Asian Languages and Civilization from the University of Chicago. For ten years she served as a professor of South Asian Studies at the University of California at Berkeley, and subsequently became Dean of the School of Arts and Sciences at Golden Gate University, San Francisco. Dr. Schomer is the author of several books and many scholarly and popular articles on history, culture, language and the arts. She is currently Provost and Institute Professor at the California Institute of Integral Studies, San Francisco.

Colophon

Typeface: Adobe Garamond
Layout: Pagemaker 6.0 for Windows
Photographs: 175 line screens from HP Scanjet 3c scans
Paper: Repap 80 lb. matte, a recycled paper